# DOWNLOADED

**Other Books by Rich Tennant**


The 5th Wave
Version 2.0: More BYTE-ing Humor from The 5th Wave

# DOWNLOADED

## THE THIRD COLLECTION OF THE 5th WAVE

### BY RICH TENNANT

**Andrews McMeel**
**Publishing**

Kansas City

00 01 02 03 04  BAH  10 9 8 7 6 5 4 3 2 1

ISBN: 0-7407-0615-2

Library of Congress Catalog Card Number: 00-103483

The 5ᵗʰ Wave may be viewed on the Internet at:
uexpress.com

To Mom—Thanks for
letting me draw
on the bathroom walls.

"Since we got it, he hasn't moved from that spot for eleven straight days. Oddly enough, they call this 'getting up and running' on the Internet."

"We can monitor our entire operation from one central location. We know what the 'Wax Lips' people are doing; we know what the 'Whoopee Cushion' people are doing; we know what the 'Fly in the Ice Cube' people are doing. But we don't know what the 'Plastic Vomit' people are doing. We don't *want* to know what the 'Plastic Vomit' people are doing."

" . . . and through image editing technology, we're able to re-create the awesome spectacle known as tyrannosaurus Gwen."

Mitch would never be sure it was laughter he heard that day at the airport, but he never again traveled with his Pez PDA.

"Well, the first day wasn't bad—I lost the 'finder,' copied a file into the 'trash,' and sat on my mouse."

Did I mention there's a balloon folding chat line on the World Wide Web?

"Remember, your Elvis should appear bald and slightly hunched—nice Big Foot, Brad—keep your two-headed animals in the shadows and your alien spacecrafts crisp and defined."

"A brief announcement class—an open-faced peanut butter sandwich is not an appropriate replacement for a missing mousepad."

"We're concerned—Kyle doesn't seem to be able to hot key between apps like all the other children."

"Fortunately at this grade level the Mac is very intuitive for them to use. Unfortunately so is sailing mousepads across the classroom."

"We pulled from several outside services to build our c/s architecture—Microsoft, Andersen Consulting, the UN peacekeeping forces. . . ."

"Now, that would show how important it is to distinguish 'fertilizing practices' from 'fertility practices' when downloading a video file from the Internet."

"It's another deep-space probe from Earth, seeking contact from extraterrestrials. I wish they'd just include an E-mail address."

"It's a free starter disk for AOL."

"Isn't that our Web master? These people always find a creative way to interface."

"It's all here, Warden. Routers, hubs, switches, all pieced together from scraps found in the machine shop. I guess the prospect of unregulated telecommunications was just too sweet to pass up."

"He should be all right now. I made him spend
two and a half hours on a 'prisoners' chat line."

"Okay, Darryl, I think it's time to admit we didn't
load the onboard mapping software correctly."

"It says, 'Thank you for downloading Gumpton's Compression Utility shareware. Should you decide to purchase this product, send a check to the address shown and your PC will be uncompressed and restored to its original size.'"

"I did this report with the help of a satellite view atmospheric map from the National Weather Service, research text from the Jet Propulsion Laboratory, and a sound file from the Barfing Lungworms' new CD."

"I don't mean to hinder your quest for knowledge; however, it's not generally a good idea to try and download the entire Internet."

"Yes, it's wireless, and yes, it weighs less than a pound, and yes, it has multiuser functionality . . . but it's a stapler."

"Before I go on to explain more advanced procedures like the zap-rowdy-students-who-don't-pay-attention function, we'll begin with some basics."

"I tell him many times—get lighter laptop. But him think he know better. Him have big ego. Him say, 'Me Tarzan, you not!' That when vine break."

"Of course graphics are important to your project, Eddy, but I think it would've been better to scan a *picture* of your worm collection."

"This is your groupware? This is what you're running?! Well heck—I think *this* could be your problem!"

"I saw the flames when they started, too.
I just thought it was part of the exhibit."

"Well! It looks like someone found the 'lion's roar'
on the sound control panel."

It started as a wrap-around porch, and then Stuart found a section on medieval architecture on the Internet.

"I found these two in the multimedia lab morphing faculty members into farm animals."

"Would you like Web or non-Web?"

"Most of our product line is doing well, but the expanding touch pad on our PDA keeps opening unexpectedly."

"Honey! Our Web browser got out last night and dumped the trash all over Mr. Belcher's home page!"

" . . . so if you have a message for someone, you write it on a
piece of paper and put it on their refrigerator with these
magnets. It's just until we get our E-mail system fixed."

"I failed her in algebra but was impressed with the way she animated her equations to dance across the screen, scream like hyenas, and then dissolve into a clip-art image of the La Brea Tar Pits."

"Clearly, the issue of middleware needs to be addressed as soon as possible."

"No, Thomas Jefferson never did 'the Grind;' however, this does show how animation can be used to illustrate American history on the Web."

"Children—it is not necessary to whisper while we're visiting the Vatican Library Web site."

"That reminds me—I installed Windows 2000
on my PC last week."

**"What do you mean you're updating our Web page?"**

IT WAS ACTUALLY ON THE WEB ONE NIGHT THAT CAPT. AHAB CAUGHT UP WITH HIS OBSESSION.

WHALE CHAT

White? Really? Where can we meet?

"Face it, Vinnie—you're gonna have a hard time getting people to subscribe on-line with a credit card to a newsletter called *Felons Interactive*."

"Yes, I'm normally larger and more awe-inspiring, but this is only a 4MB system!"

"They're fruit flies, Rog. For gosh sake, how many Applets have you written today?!"

"I think the cursor's not moving, Mr. Dunt, because you've got your hand on the chalk board eraser and not the mouse."

THE NEW HOLLYWOOD

CUT! PASTE!

"I don't care if you *do* have a coalition of kids from nineteen countries backing you up; I'm still not buying you an ISDN line."

46

"Our classroom PCs have created a challenging atmosphere where critical analyzing, synthesizing, and problem-solving skills are honed. I think the students have gotten a lot out of them, too."

47

"If I'm not gaining weight, then why does this digital image take up 3MB more memory than a comparable one taken six months ago?"

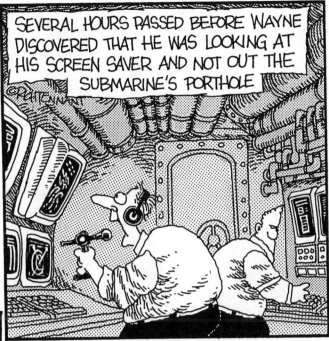

"It's *incredible*! I'm seeing life forms never before imagined!! Bizarre, colorful, almost whimsical!!!"

"Well, shoot! This eggplant chart is just as confusing as the butternut squash chart and the gourd chart. Can't you just make a pie chart like everyone else?"

"I asked for software that would biodegrade after it was thrown out, not while it was running."

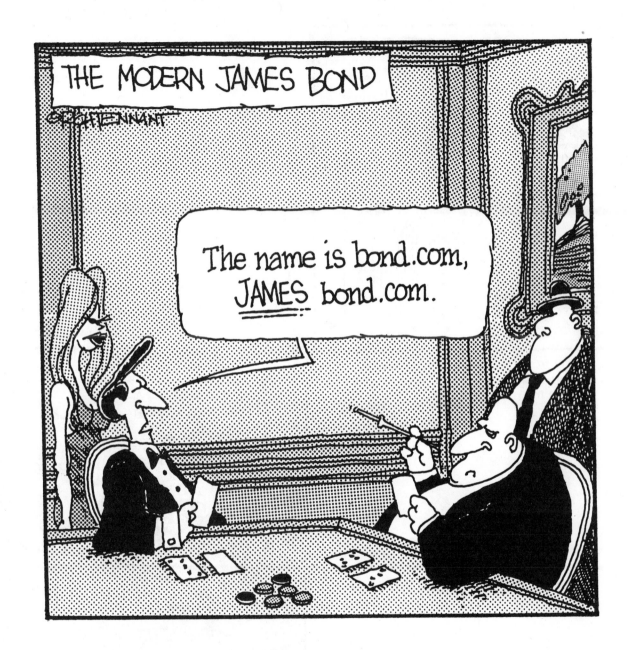

"It's a letter from the company that installed our in-ground sprinkler system. They're offering Internet access now."

WELL, OBVIOUSLY ONE OF THE CELLS IN THE NAVIGATIONAL SPREADSHEET IS CORRUPT!

"I couldn't get this 'job skills' program to work on my PC, so I replaced the motherboard, upgraded the BIOS, and wrote a program that links it to my personal database. It told me I wasn't technically inclined and should pursue a career in sales."

"From now on, let's confine our exploration of ancient Egypt to the computer program."

"It's just until we get back up on the Internet."

"My girlfriend ran a spreadsheet of my life and generated this chart. My best hope is that she'll change her major from 'computer sciences' to 'rehabilitative services.'"

"I'm not sure I like a college whose home page has a link to the Party Zone!"

"It's a ten-step word processing program. It comes with a spell checker, grammar checker, cliché checker, whine checker, passive/aggressive checker, politically correct checker, hissy fit checker, pretentious pontificating checker, boring anecdote checker, and a Freudian reference checker."

"I couldn't say anything—they were in here with that program we bought them that encourages artistic expression."

"She just found out she'd rather be a jet pilot than a fairy princess, but she doesn't want to give up the wardrobe."

"We're researching molecular/digital technology that moves massive amounts of information across binary pathways that interact with free-agent programs capable of making decisions and performing logical tasks. We see applications in really high-end doorbells."

"It's a football/math program. We're tackling multiplication, going long for division, and punting fractions."

"... and you say a giant has your mother and father locked in a dungeon? And your sister's being held hostage in a tower? You just sit tight, Davey—a SWAT team is on its way."

DAD ADDS MULTIMEDIA SOUND AND GRAPHICS TO THE TRADITIONAL CAMPFIRE GHOST STORY.

"Sales on the Web site are down. I figure the server's chi is blocked, so we're fudgin' around the feng shui in the computer room, and if that doesn't work, Ronnie's got a chant that should do it."

"Well heck, all the boy did was launch a search on the Web and up comes Tracy's retainer, your car keys, and my bowling trophy here on a site in Seattle."

"Tell the boss he's got more flame mail from you-know-who."

"I don't care what your E-mail friends in Europe say, you're not having a glass of Chianti with your bologna sandwich."

"I don't know how it happened, but there's an applet in the toaster and some guy in Norway keeps burning my toast."

"Well, this is festive—a miniature intranet
amidst a swirl of Java applets."

"That reminds me—I have to figure out how to
install our CD-ROM and external hard drive."

"This afternoon I want everyone to go on-line and find all you can about Native American culture, history of the Old West, and discount airfares to Hawaii for the two weeks I'll be on vacation."

Mr. Grady had a way of getting more out of an on-line project than other teachers.

Ms. Stubb's 7th Grade Class
CLOGGING in Squash Carving

Mr Grady's 6th Grade Class
GLOBAL ECONOMIC STABILITY

"Give him air! Give him air! He'll be okay. He's just been exposed to some raw HTML code. It must have accidently flashed across his screen from the server."

"Okay—antidote, antidote, what would an antidote icon look like? You know, I still haven't got this desktop the way I want it."

"Great goulash, Stan. That reminds me, are you still scripting your own Web page?"

"All I'm going to say is, be very careful assigning projects around the 'ancient tribal rites' Web page."

"Oh, well shoot! Must be that new paint program on my HPC."

"Okay, I think I forgot to mention this, but we now have a Web management function that automatically alerts us when there's a broken link on the Aquarium's Web site."

"... and I'd also like to thank Doug Gretzel here for all his work in helping us develop our interactive, multimedia stapling division."

"Look, I've already launched a search for 'reanimated babe cadavers' *three times* and nothing came up!"

" . . . and here's me with Cindy Crawford. And this is me with Madonna and Celine Dion. . . ."

"Ronnie made the body from what he learned in metal shop, Sissy and Darlene's home ec class helped them in fixing up the inside, and then all that antigravity stuff we picked up off the Web."

"Oh jeez! I hate when you fish out toasted chips with a butter knife!"

"You're a great geek, Martin. You're just not my geek."

"We're not sure what it is. Rob cobbled it together from paper clips and stuff in the mail room, but *man*, wait till you see how scalable it is."

"Well, there goes the simple charm of sitting around the stove surfing the Web on our laptops."

"Great! It comes with Quicken. Now maybe we can figure out where all the money around here is going."

"I'm just not sure it's appropriate to send a digital resume to a paper stock company looking for a sales rep."

"It's a Weber PalmPit Pro handheld barbecue with 24 btu, rechargable battery pack, and applications for roasting, smoking, and open-flame cooking."

Maintenance is chagrined to find out the squeak in Clark's disk drive is really a whistle in Clark's nose.

78

"The new technology has really helped me get organized. I keep my project reports under the PC, budgets under my laptop, and memos under my pager."

"Hold on there, boy! You think you're gonna install Windows 2000 on old '386' yourself? Well you'd better hope to high heaven she's in a good mood today."

"Just how accurately should my Web site reflect my place of business?"

"Your database is beyond repair, but before I tell you our back-up recommendation, let me ask you a question. How many index cards do you think will fit on the walls of your computer room?"

"You know, I've asked you a dozen times *not* to animate the torches on our Web page."

"You're not going to believe this, but I'm standing in front of a 14.4K chimney. I'll be here all night downloading this stuff."

**"Oddly enough it came with a PCI bus slot."**

"Brad! That's not your modem we're hearing! It's Buddy!! He's out of his cage and in the iMac!!"

Now maybe these folks got a decent disaster recovery plan and maybe they don't...

DANGER
WILD RHINOCEROS

"What is it, Lassie? Is it Gramps? Is it his hard disk? Is he stuck somewhere, girl? Is he trying to write CGI programs to a Unix server running VRML? What, girl, what?!"

"Oh yeah, he's got a lot of money. When he tries to check his balance on-line, he gets a computer message saying there's insufficient memory to complete the task."

"We're much better prepared for this upgrade than before. We're giving users additional training, better manuals, and a morphine drip."

"As a candidate for network administrator, how well versed are you in remote connectivity protocols?"

"I guess you could say this is the
hub of our network."

"It's a wonderful idea, Ralph. But do you really think 'AnnoyPersonTP' and "DumbMemoTP" will work as protocols on our TCP/IP suite?"

NETWORK+ EXAM

"I'm not sure you're taking this exam seriously enough. When asked to give a description of a 'repeater,' you wrote the recipe for a large bean burrito."

"You can do a lot with a handheld computing device, and I guess dressing one up in G.I. Joe clothes and calling it your little desk commander is okay, too."

I'M JUST HAVING TROUBLE DATING A GUY WHOSE NAME DEFAULTS TO "LOONY FRUITCAKE" ON MY SPELL CHECKER.

"Do you have one with a longer antenna?"

" . . . and Bobby here found a way to extend our data transmission an additional 3,000 meters using coax cable. How'd you do that, Bobby—repeaters?"

"I think you've made a mistake. We do photo retouching, not family portraits . . . oooh, wait a minute—I think I get it!"

"I don't know what program you been usin', Frank, but it ain't the right one. Look—your menu bar should read, File, Edit, Reap, Gather . . ."

"Yeah, these voice recognition systems can be tricky. Let me see if I can open your word processing program."

"No, Stuart, I won't look up 'rampaging elephants' on the Web. We're studying plant life, and right now, photosynthesis is a more pertinent topic."

"That's a lovely scanned image of your sister's portrait. Now take it off the body of that pit viper before she comes in the room."

"You know, I'll never get used to that exploding
bomb error message icon!"

SINCE THEN WE DISCONNECT
THE ONLINE SHOPPING
FUNCTION DURING THE HOURS
"LIFESTYLES OF THE RICH AND
FAMOUS" IS ON.

"Maybe it would help our Web site if we showed our products in action."

"Come on Walt—time to freshen
the company Web page."

"They were selling illegal substances on-line. We
broke through the door just as they were trying to
flush the hardrive down the toilet."

"You know, it dawned on me last night why we aren't getting any hits on our Web site."

"Right here . . . crimeorg.com. It says the well-run small criminal concern should have no more than nine goons, six henchmen, and four stooges. Right now, I think we're goon heavy."

"So far our Web presence has been pretty good. We've gotten some orders, a few inquiries, and nine guys who want to date our logo."

"I like getting complaint letters by E-mail. It's easier to delete than to shred."

"I have to say I'm really impressed with the interactivity on this car-wash Web site."

"So, what kind of roaming capabilities
does this thing have?"

"You'd better come out here—I've got someone
who wants to run a banner ad on our Web site."

"Remember—I want the bleeding file server surrounded by flaming workstations with the word 'Motherboard' scrolling underneath."

"Sometimes I feel behind the times. I asked my eleven-year-old to build a Web site for my business, and he said he would, only after he finishes the one he's building for his ant farm."

"You the guy having trouble staying connected
to the network?"

110

"I assume you'll be forward thinking enough to allow '.dog' as a valid domain name."

"Troubleshooting's a little tricky here. The route table to our destination hosts include a Morse code key, several walkie-talkies, and a guy with nine messenger pigeons."

"I'm not saying I believe in anything. All I know is since it's been there our server is running 50 percent faster."

"... and it doesn't appear that you'll have much trouble grasping some of the more 'alien' configuration concepts on this MCSE exam."

Despite its inclusion on the Hardware Compatability List, Martin shuddered at the thought of having to install Windows NT on the workstation from the early 1950s.

"Okay, make sure this is right. 'Looking for caring companion who likes old movies, nature walks, and quiet evenings at home. Knowledge of configuring a 32-bit Microsoft Client for NetWare Networks in Windows 98 a plus.'"

"The first thing you should know about investing on-line is that when you see the exploding bomb icon appear, it's just your browser crashing—not your portfolio."

"Sure, at first it sounded great—an intuitive
network adapter that helps people write memos
by finishing their thoughts for them."

"If it works, it works. I've just never seen
network cabling connected with
Chinese handcuffs before."

"One of the first things you want to do before
installing NT Server is fog the users to keep them
calm during the procedure."

**"We sort of have our own way of mentally preparing our people to take the MCSE NT Workstation exam."**

"Before the Internet, we were only bustin' chops locally. But now, with our Web site, we're bustin' chops all over the world."

"I'm not sure a fantasy sports Web site for professional wrestling would work. Professional wrestling is already a fantasy sport."

"Oh wait—this says, '*Lunch* Ed from Marketing,' not 'Lynch,' '*Lunch*.'"

"I understand how the thumb is the pointing device, but why does *this* finger have to be the antenna?"

". . . and then one day it hit Tarzan, Lord of Jungle—where future in that?"

"I've got some image editing software, so I took the liberty of erasing some of the smudges that kept showing up around the clouds, no need to thank me."

I located the bear and began testing the vibrating tracking collar over a week ago, but he seems to have left the cave and now I can't locate him <u>or</u> the collar anywhere.

"Come here, quick! I've got a new iMac trick!"

"This part of the test tells us whether you're personally suited to the job of network administrator."

"I ran this Bob Dylan CD through our voice recognition system, and he really is just saying, 'Manaamamanaaabadhaabadha . . .'"

"Room service? Please send someone up to refresh the mini bar, make up the room, and defrag the hard drive."

"Look at that craftsmanship. Notice the patina. It's already three years old. In the computer industry, that makes it a genuine antique."

"I think my body's energy centers *are* well balanced. I keep my pager on my belt, my cell phone in my right pocket, and my palmtop computer in my inside left breast pocket."

127

"So far he's called up a cobra, two pythons, and a bunch of skinks, but still not the file we're looking for."

"Well, here's what happened—I forgot to
put it on my to-do list."

"I tell you, it looks like Danny, it sounds like Danny, but it's *not* Danny!! I think the Mac has created an alias of Danny! You can see it in his eyes—little wristwatch icons!"

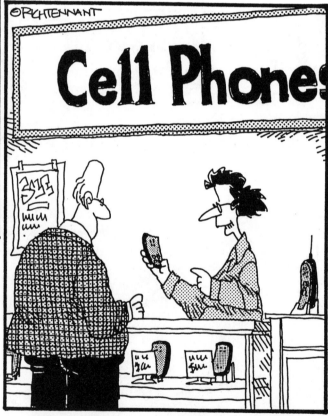

"This model comes with a particularly useful function—the simulated static button for breaking out of long-winded, meaningless conversations."

"I'm not sure—I like the mutual funds with rotating dollar signs, although the dancing stocks and bonds look good, too."

"Well, that's the third one in as many clicks. I'm sure it's just a coincidence, still, don't use the 'launcher' again until I've had a look at it."

THE NEXT EVOLUTION IN PALM-TOP ORGANIZERS

# The PatchPilot

Delivers a preset amount of data into your bloodstream which quickly rushes it to your brain and subconscious.

I have to go now. I suddenly got the feeling I'm supposed to be at a meeting in 10 minutes.

"I know my modem's in the microwave. It seems to increase transmission speed. Can you punch in 'defrost'? I have a lot of E-mails going out."

"You ever get the feeling this project could just up and die at any moment?"

"We take network security very seriously here."

"You know, this was a situation question on my Network exam, but I always thought it was just hypothetical."

"The kids are getting up right now. When we wired the house we added vibrating pager technology to their bunk beds."

"Oh, that's Jack's area for his paper crafts. He's made some wonderful U.S. Treasury Bonds, certificates of deposit, $20s, $50s, $100s, that sort of thing."

"It's okay. One of the routers must have gone down and we had a brief broadcast storm."

**WIRED HOME OF THE FUTURE**

@RICHTENNANT

"I'm setting preferences—do you want Oriental or Persian carpets in the living room?"

**EXPERIMENTING WITH THE WIRELESS LASER BEAM NETWORK**

@RICHTENNANT

"Okay—did you get that?"

"It's called 'Linux Poker.' Everyone gets to see everyone else's cards, everything's wild, you can play off your opponents' hands, and everyone wins excepts Bill Gates, whose face appears on the Jokers."

139

# WHEN POWER USERS WANT PERFORMANCE AND FUN, THEY TURN TO THE...

## HiJinx Interactive Workstation

17" FunHouse monitor distorts and bends your files into interesting and engaging documents

6.4GB hard disk has Squirting Flower processor

AirJet Keyboard sends hats, wigs & toupees flying around the room

JoyBuzzer trackball keeps users howling

©RICHTENNANT

"Our automated response policy to a large company-wide data crash is to notify management, back up existing data, and sell 90 percent of my shares in the company."

"You might want to adjust the value of your 'nudge' function."

"Philip—come quick! David just used Slackware
to connect the amp and speakers
to his air guitar!"

IT WAS KEVIN'S FIRST ATTEMPT AT INSTALLING GHOSTSCRIPT. AN ICY CHILL WENT DOWN HIS SPINE AS HIS OUIJA BOARD SUDDENLY FELL FROM THE SHELF CAUSING HIS CANDLE TO FLICKER WILDLY

"It's been two days, Larry. It's time to stop enjoying the new-computer smell and take the iMac out of the box."

"So much for the graffiti handwriting system."